Forces and Motion:
INVESTIGATING A CAR CRASH

Ian Graham

Raintree

Raintree is an imprint of Capstone Global Library Limited, a company incorporated in England and Wales having its registered office at 7 Pilgrim Street, London, EC4V 6LB – Registered company number: 6695582

www.raintreepublishers.co.uk
myorders@raintreepublishers.co.uk.

Text © Capstone Global Library Limited 2014
First published in hardback in 2014
Paperback edition first published in 2015
The moral rights of the proprietor have been asserted.

Edited by Andrew Farrow, Adam Miller, and Adrian Vigliano
Designed by Richard Parker
Original illustrations © HL Studios
Illustrated by James Stayte (pages 4–7); HL Studios
Picture research by Ruth Blair
Production by Sophia Argyris
Originated by Capstone Global Library Ltd
Printed and bound in China by CTPS

ISBN 978 1 406 26103 5 (hardback)
17 16 15 14 13
10 9 8 7 6 5 4 3 2 1

ISBN 978 1 406 26109 7 (paperback)
18 17 16 15 14
10 9 8 7 6 5 4 3 2 1

British Library Cataloguing in Publication Data
Graham, Ian
Forces and motion: investigating a car crash. – (Anatomy of an investigation)

A full catalogue record for this book is available from the British Library.

Acknowledgements

We would like to thank the following for permission to reproduce photographs: Alamy pp. 18 (© Paul Bernhardt), 21 (© Simon Price), 34 (© Transtock Inc.), 36 (© Wildlife GmbH); Corbis pp. 30 (© Timothy Fadek), 31 (© Paul Thompson), 40 (© Corbis), 42 (© Image Source); Getty Images pp. 10 (John Walker/Fresno Bee/MCT), 13 (Philippe Merle/AFP), 15 (Nasa), 25 (Rolf Vennenbernd/AFP), 27 (Jack Hardmann/Bloomberg), 43 (Haruyoshi Yamaguchi/Bloomberg), 49 (Robert Cianflone); iStockphoto pp. 17 (© CountryStyle Photography), 32 (© Maxim Malevich), 41 (© Colleen Butler); Science Photo Library pp. 23 (Mauro Fermariello), 24 (Michael Donne), 28 (Robert Brook); Shutterstock pp. 8 (© Dedyukhin Dmitry), 9 (© TFoxFoto), 19 (© Brad Thompson), 29 (© Tramper), 33 (© Amy Johansson), 35 (© oksana.perkins), 39 (© S_E), 45 (© azharjggt); Superstock p. 22 (Marka).

Cover photograph of a police investigator looking over a seven car accident reproduced with permission of Alamy (© ZUMA Wire Service).

We would like to thank Rob Newton for his invaluable help in the preparation of this book.

Every effort has been made to contact copyright holders of any material reproduced in this book. Any omissions will be rectified in subsequent printings if notice is given to the publisher.

Disclaimer
All the internet addresses (URLs) given in this book were valid at the time of going to press. However, due to the dynamic nature of the internet, some addresses may have changed, or sites may have changed or ceased to exist since publication. While the author and publisher regret any inconvenience this may cause readers, no responsibility for any such changes can be accepted by either the author or the publisher.

Contents

Some words are printed in bold, **like this**. You can find out what they mean by looking in the glossary on page 52.

CRASH!

Pedestrians hurry along, while traffic passes by unnoticed □ until...

What was that?

Vehicles are turning, skidding, and crashing into each other. A lorry slides sideways across the road.

People start calling emergency services on their mobile phones.

There's been an accident on Main Street.

Police cars, fire engines, and ambulances race to the scene of the collision.

There is an eerie silence after the crash. It happened so fast that no one is certain what caused it. Dazed drivers and passengers begin emerging from some of the vehicles. A few pedestrians run to help them. Someone is trapped in a car that has crashed into the back of the lorry. Within a few minutes, the sound of sirens can be heard in the distance. Professional help is on the way.

Several vehicles have crashed into each other. Luckily, no one has died, but several people are injured, and at least one driver is trapped in his car.

Some police officers close the road; others ask witnesses what they saw and heard. Meanwhile, paramedics treat minor injuries and begin taking more seriously injured people to hospital.

Did you see what happened?

Firefighters cut the roof off a car to release the driver trapped inside.

Look at this.

Hmmm, this is interesting.

While the emergency services make the accident scene safe and tend to the injured, accident investigators arrive and begin the task of working out what caused the crash. The accident scene is a giant puzzle of tangled vehicles. It contains clues and evidence that investigators will use to help them understand the forces involved in the crash and the motion of the vehicles so that they can reveal the story of what happened. Now, a detailed investigation begins...

First steps

When emergency services arrive at a road accident, their first priority is saving lives and treating injuries. People may need to be cut out of damaged vehicles, because the **forces** of the **collision** have changed the shape of the vehicles and jammed the doors shut.

Most vehicles are made of steel, because steel is easy to bend into the shape of a vehicle. But this useful **property** means that vehicles are also bent out of shape easily by the forces involved in a crash.

When a vehicle crashes, the force of the collision bends and breaks parts of the vehicle. This red arrow shows the direction of the force that damaged this car.

What are forces?

In science, forces are pushes or pulls that change an object's speed, direction, or shape. Forces have size and direction. Scientists describe quantities like this as **vectors**.

Forces make vehicles move, change direction, and stop. They also bend and break parts of vehicles during a crash. Rescue workers use powerful tools such as the **Jaws of Life**, which produce the huge forces needed to bend metal or cut through it at the scene of an accident in order to rescue people.

PRESSURE

Pressure is the pushing effect of a force acting on a surface. It is measured by dividing the force by the area of the surface. The pressure inside a car tyre is just over twice the outside air pressure. The Jaws of Life tools used by rescue workers are operated by high-pressure, fire-resistant liquid at up to 350 times normal air pressure.

YOU'RE THE INVESTIGATOR!

You are called to the scene of an accident. No one has been hurt. Only one car is involved. A car has hit a postbox on the pavement and knocked it over. The driver, who is yawning a lot, says a child ran out in front of him. He says he swerved to avoid the child and skidded across the dry road onto the pavement. How can you find out if the driver is telling the truth? (You can find the answer on page 11.)

Rescue workers can use powerful Jaws of Life tools to open up the body of a crashed car. One of these tools has powerful cutting jaws that can slice through metal like a hot knife through butter. Other tools have spreading jaws or pushers to pry parts of a car open.

Protect the scene

The crash scene is full of **evidence** that accident investigators can use to find out what caused the accident. Investigators must make sure the whole scene is protected, so that other vehicles cannot drive into it and cause more injuries and damage – or perhaps destroy valuable evidence. Police and other emergency service workers may close the road or, if part of the road can be kept open, they set out traffic cones to keep other vehicles at a safe distance.

A major accident may involve dozens of collisions between many vehicles. Untangling the events that caused the accident can be a very complex problem for accident investigators to solve.

Police officers treat a serious traffic accident as a potential crime scene. They may give a breath test to drivers to find out if any of them have been drinking alcohol. Drivers may be given drug tests, too. Police officers take the details of everyone present and take statements from them about what happened. They also check that none of the vehicles has been stolen and that the drivers all have the proper **insurance**.

Crumple zones

Some parts of a vehicle are designed to bend, or crumple, in a crash. They are called **crumple zones**. When they crumple, they absorb some of the forces and **energy** of the crash and therefore protect people inside the vehicle. Crumple zones can be built into any part of a vehicle, but they are most common at the front, because more than half of all impacts affect the front of a vehicle.

Rear crumple zone

Front crumple zone

Crumple zones are designed to bend and buckle in a crash. A car with crumple zones looks terrible after a crash, but if you look closely, you will see that the part where passengers sit is undamaged.

YOU'RE THE INVESTIGATOR!: THE ANSWER

Look back at the box on page 9. You carefully examine the road. There are no skid marks. What does it mean? The driver said the car skidded across the road. If there are no skid marks, the driver could not have been braking hard enough to make the car skid. The driver's story is not true. The driver seems to be very tired, because he cannot stop yawning. It is more likely that he fell asleep at the wheel, and then the car ran off the road.

Why investigate accidents?

As a result of road accidents worldwide, about 1.3 million people die and up to 50 million people are injured each year. It is important to know how and why these accidents happen. That way, if there are any common causes, experts can deal with them by improving vehicle technology, altering road layouts, or changing the laws that relate to driving. The results of investigations may help to prevent future accidents. Discovering how people are injured also helps to improve the design of car safety features such as bumpers, seat belts, airbags, and collapsible steering wheels so that they give more protection to drivers, passengers, and **pedestrians**.

Crash investigations can help with legal cases by finding out if anyone involved in a road accident has broken the law. Insurance companies may also use the facts from investigations to settle claims.

Police officers investigate most road accidents, but it is also becoming increasingly common for professional accident investigators to be called in. These experts enable police officers to concentrate on policing duties, and they bring a wealth of scientific and technical expertise to accident investigations.

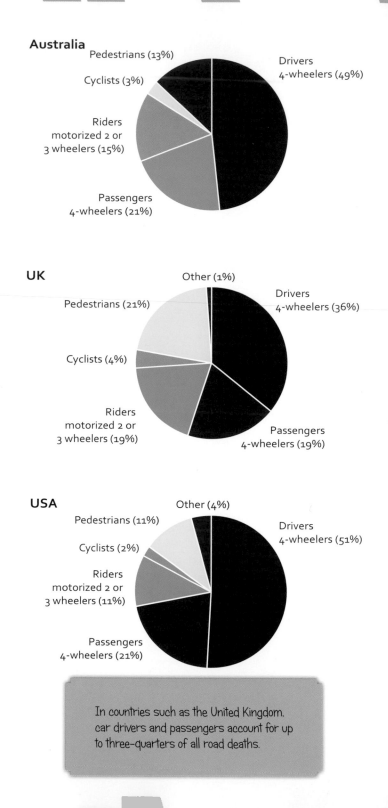

Australia
Pedestrians (13%)
Cyclists (3%)
Riders motorized 2 or 3 wheelers (15%)
Passengers 4-wheelers (21%)
Drivers 4-wheelers (49%)

UK
Other (1%)
Pedestrians (21%)
Cyclists (4%)
Riders motorized 2 or 3 wheelers (19%)
Drivers 4-wheelers (36%)
Passengers 4-wheelers (19%)

USA
Other (4%)
Pedestrians (11%)
Cyclists (2%)
Riders motorized 2 or 3 wheelers (11%)
Passengers 4-wheelers (21%)
Drivers 4-wheelers (51%)

In countries such as the United Kingdom, car drivers and passengers account for up to three-quarters of all road deaths.

SPEED AND VELOCITY

Moving vehicles have speed and **velocity**. Speed is a number that shows how fast a vehicle is going. Velocity shows how fast a vehicle is going in a particular direction. Speed is a scalar quantity (a number without direction). Velocity is a vector quantity (a number with direction).

Accident investigators work for police forces, solicitors, and insurance companies. They may be called to the scene of an accident as soon as the emergency services are alerted, or they may be consulted days or weeks later. If they are called in after the accident scene has been cleared, they examine the vehicles that were involved in the accident and use photographs taken at the time of the accident and measurements made by police officers. They are particularly interested in finding out the speed and direction of every vehicle just before the accident.

Investigators and rescue workers discuss their observations at the scene of a road accident.

CRASH INVESTIGATOR

Crash investigators try to work out why an accident happened.

Professional crash investigators normally have a degree in **physics** or **engineering** or a background in repairing accident-damaged vehicles. They could also be former police officers with experience in investigating road accidents. They have specialized training in accident investigation and reconstruction.

How an accident is investigated

Investigators start with what they know, and then they carefully work out how the vehicles involved in a collision ended up in their final resting places. The investigators collect evidence and take measurements from the accident scene. Then they use scientific **analysis**, mathematical **formulae**, and experience gained from investigating many other accidents to develop a **hypothesis**, or explanation, for the series of events that led to the accident and what happened during the collision itself, called the impact phase.

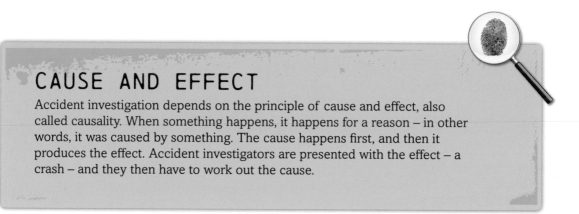

CAUSE AND EFFECT

Accident investigation depends on the principle of cause and effect, also called causality. When something happens, it happens for a reason – in other words, it was caused by something. The cause happens first, and then it produces the effect. Accident investigators are presented with the effect – a crash – and they then have to work out the cause.

Case studies: crash courses

All the measurements that an accident investigator makes must be in the same system of units. The loss of the Mars Climate Orbiter spacecraft in 1999 showed what can happen if different units are mixed up. NASA's ground controllers lost contact with the spacecraft after it changed course to go into orbit around the planet Mars. The orbiter passed behind Mars 49 seconds earlier than expected and could not be contacted again.

Accident investigators found that the spacecraft's software expected the information controlling its engines to be given in metric units, but engineers sent the information to the spacecraft in non-metric (imperial) units. This resulted in the multi-million dollar spacecraft following the wrong course, passing too close to Mars, and breaking up in the atmosphere. This incident has been called the "metric mix-up".

A mix-up in units also caused a Boeing 767 airliner to run out of fuel during a flight in 1983, because not enough fuel had been loaded. The crew of Air Canada Flight 143 was able to glide the plane over 30 kilometres (over 20 miles) to a former airfield and land safely. None of the crew or passengers was hurt during the unpowered landing.

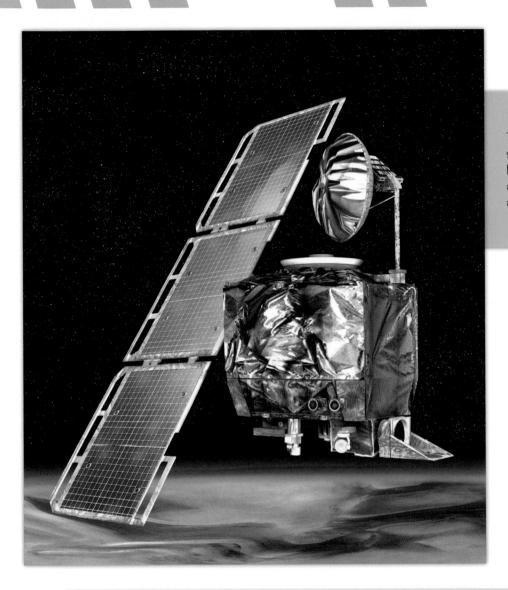

The Mars Climate Orbiter spacecraft crashed on Mars in 1999 because of a mix-up between metric and non-metric units.

MEASUREMENTS AND UNITS

The metric system of units is used throughout most of the world. Distance is measured in metres and speed is measured in metres per second or kilometres per hour. Some countries use a different system, with distance measured in feet and speed measured in feet per second or miles per hour. In the UK, we use metric and non-metric measurements. Metric and non-metric measurements should never be used together in the same calculation.

Forces and energy

Investigators use mathematical formulae to **analyse** accidents. This is because moving vehicles obey the laws of physics, including Newton's laws of motion and the conservation of energy and **momentum**.

Newton's laws of motion

Newton's laws of motion (named after scientist Isaac Newton) predict how objects, including cars, move when forces act on them. Newton's three laws of motion state that:

1. An object stays at rest or keeps going in a straight line at a constant speed unless a force acts on it.
2. When a force makes an object **accelerate**, the **acceleration** is proportional to the force. This means that a bigger force produces faster acceleration.
3. When two objects exert force on each other, the action and reaction forces are equal in magnitude and opposite in direction. This means that a force acting on an object produces an equal force acting in the opposite direction.

In practice, this means that objects, including cars, do not start moving unless a force acts on them. Once they start moving, they do not change speed or direction unless a force acts on them. Bigger forces produce bigger changes in speed and direction.

Whether a vehicle is a small sports car, a bulky SUV, or a heavily loaded lorry, the same forces act on it.

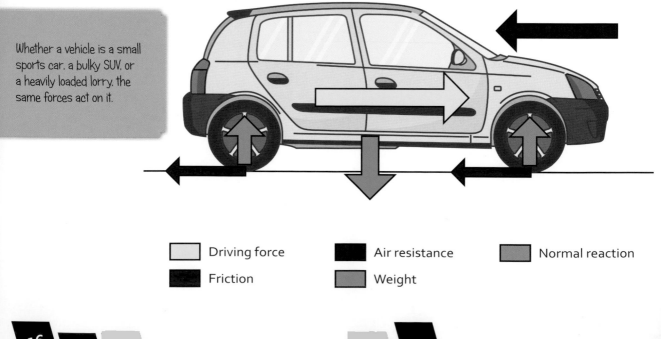

	Driving force		Air resistance		Normal reaction
	Friction		Weight		

FORCES IN ACTION

The forces that act on a moving vehicle are:

- the driving force produced by a vehicle's engine turning two or more of the wheels
- friction between its tyres and the ground
- the vehicle's **weight** due to **gravity**, acting downwards
- the normal force of the ground acting upwards against the car
- air resistance, or drag.

Balanced and unbalanced forces

When a vehicle stands still, the forces acting on it are balanced. The vehicle's weight acts downwards against the ground. This is balanced by an equal and opposite force, called the **normal force**, acting upwards on the vehicle. When the driver starts the engine and begins to move, the force of the wheels pushing back against the ground is greater than the **friction** (see the box) and **drag** forces that resist movement. These unbalanced forces result in a forward force, which makes the vehicle accelerate.

Ice makes roads slippery, because it reduces the friction between a car's tyres and the road. Lorries spread coarse sand on icy roads to increase the friction between the tyres and the road, giving the tyres more grip (see page 37).

Friction: good or bad?

Friction is a force that tries to stop objects from sliding across each other. It can be very useful. Friction between the ground and a vehicle's tyres give the tyres something to push against and enables the vehicle to move and steer. But friction can also be damaging. Friction between the moving parts of a machine, such as a car engine, causes wear.

Motion and energy

There is another way to think about moving vehicles and collisions. Instead of forces, accident investigators can think about the energy of the vehicles. Moving vehicles have a type of energy called **kinetic energy** (see the box). This energy is transferred to other vehicles and objects in a crash. This is why faster vehicles – with more energy – cause more damage when they crash.

When a driver brakes, a vehicle slows down, and it therefore loses kinetic energy. Where does this energy go? It changes into heat in the brakes. The brakes work by squeezing tough pads together to grip a disc connected to each wheel. Friction between the pads and disc slows down the vehicle and produces a lot of heat, which radiates (moves) away into the air.

The brakes of very fast cars that brake hard and often. such as racing cars. get so hot that they glow red-hot.

WHAT IS ENERGY?

Energy is the ability to do work. Energy can never be created or destroyed, but it can be changed from one form to another. There are two main types of energy: kinetic energy and potential energy. Kinetic energy is the energy something has because it is moving. Potential energy is the energy something has because of its position or state. Electrical energy and gravitational energy are examples of potential energy.

THE MATHS OF ENERGY

The **equation** used to calculate the kinetic energy of a vehicle is:

Kinetic energy = ½ m v²   m = the vehicle's **mass** in kilograms
                                     v = vehicle's speed in metres per second

Kinetic energy depends on a vehicle's mass and the square of its speed. So, if a vehicle's speed doubles, it has four times the kinetic energy. Let's show this with a simple calculation.

Imagine a car with a mass of 1,500 kg is travelling at 40 kilometres per hour (kph). A speed of 40 kph is roughly the same as 11 metres per second. So, the car's kinetic energy is calculated as follows:

  ½ x 1,500 x 11 x 11 = 90,750 joules

If the speed doubles to 80 kph (22 metres per second), the car's kinetic energy is calculated as follows:

  ½ x 1,500 x 22 x 22 = 363,000 joules

Energy is required to bend metal. In a collision, the energy that causes all the damage is supplied by the kinetic energy of the moving vehicles.

Conservation laws

Colliding vehicles obey the laws of physics. A crash between vehicles is a bit like a game of pool. When a vehicle collides with something, it gives up some or all of its energy to whatever it hits. Energy is transferred from vehicle to vehicle, and it changes from one form to another – from kinetic energy to heat and sound, for example.

The energy of all the vehicles and objects involved in a collision obey a law of physics called the law of conservation of energy. All the energy of the vehicles immediately before they crash into each other equals all the energy of the vehicles immediately after they have crashed. However, the energy may be spread out differently among the vehicles after the crash.

Moving vehicles have another property called momentum. A moving vehicle's momentum is its mass multiplied by its velocity (see the diagram).

> The total momentum of two vehicles before a crash equals the total momentum of the two vehicles after the crash.

Before collision

| 1,500 kg | 1,000 kg | Total momentum |
| 20 metres/second | 10 metres/second | 40,000 kg m/s |

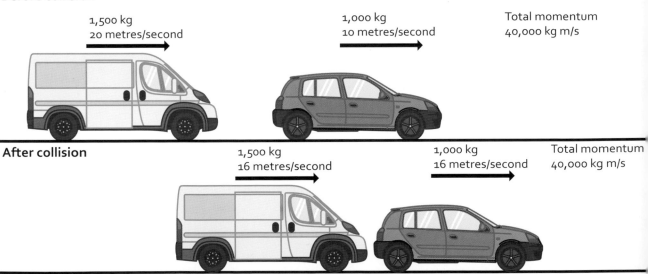

After collision

| 1,500 kg | 1,000 kg | Total momentum |
| 16 metres/second | 16 metres/second | 40,000 kg m/s |

Momentum is conserved in a collision, too. These laws that link force, energy, momentum, speed, mass, and **inertia** (see the box on page 21) allow an accident investigator to calculate what happened to vehicles before they collided.

Inertia

All vehicles have mass. It is the amount of matter, or "stuff", they contain. The more mass an object is made of, the more difficult it is to make the object move, and the more difficult it is to stop it again. This property is called inertia.

A heavily loaded, moving lorry has more kinetic energy, momentum, and inertia than a small car. This makes the lorry more dangerous and damaging in a collision.

YOU'RE THE INVESTIGATOR!

A white car has crashed into a wall. The car is badly damaged. The front crumpled after colliding with the wall. There are blue streaks and scrapes down to the bare metal along one side of the car. Something is missing from this scene that is very important in the accident investigation. What is it? (See page 23 for the answer.)

Collision forces

When a vehicle stops suddenly because of a collision, the people in the vehicle keep going at the same speed in the same direction for a moment – until they hit something inside the vehicle. The hard parts of the human body, especially the rib cage and skull, stop instantly when they hit a surface. This possibly causes fractures, and soft organs can crush against them, resulting in serious internal injuries in people involved in crashes.

Safety measures are built into cars that try to prevent this in two ways. First, seat belts hold people in their seats so that they do not fly forwards and hit the inside of the car. Second, soft materials inside the car slow down the process of people hitting them and cushion the impact.

Seat belts

Wearing a seat belt reduces the risk of death for front-seat passengers by up to 65 per cent, and it reduces the risk of death for back-seat passengers by up to 75 per cent. However, laws requiring front-seat and back-seat passengers to wear seat belts exist in only 57 per cent of countries.

Since the 1970s, some cars have been fitted with airbags. If a car stops suddenly in a collision, a bag hidden inside the steering wheel instantly blows up with gas to form a soft cushion that catches the driver's head. Some cars also have airbags for passengers as well as side-impact airbags.

When a car crashes into something, the driver's head is slowed to a halt more gently and safely by an airbag than it would be by coming to a sudden halt when striking the steering wheel.

YOU'RE THE INVESTIGATOR!: THE ANSWER

Look back at the box on page 21. The blue scrapes on fresh damage suggest that a blue vehicle struck the white car. This blue vehicle is what is missing from the accident scene. Some of the paint from the blue vehicle was transferred to the white car, causing the blue streaks, but the driver did not stop. Why did the driver leave? Perhaps the car was stolen or uninsured, or maybe the driver was drunk or did not have a licence.

Experts collect traces of paint from a vehicle involved in a collision. Investigators can analyse the layers of different colours and chemicals in the tiny paint flakes to identify the model of vehicle they came from.

Collecting data

Investigators called to the scene of an accident arrive within a few minutes. They report to the officer in charge and make sure the scene is safe and that the investigation won't hinder the rescue of casualties. Their next priority is to preserve and record as much evidence as possible. They first examine the most fragile evidence, such as pools of fuel that will evaporate quickly and disappear. They measure and photograph this kind of evidence.

INFORMATION GATHERING

Accident investigators gather information about:

- the points on the road where vehicles collided, which are marked by broken glass and other debris
- skid marks, fluid trails, and scuff marks on the road caused by contact between the road and vehicles and wheels
- the location and severity of damage on vehicles
- damage to lampposts, postboxes, rubbish bins, signs, barriers, kerbs, trees, and other fixed objects
- obstructions (things that block a view), distractions (things that divert attention), or anything that might have affected the drivers' view of the road
- the state of airbags, seat belts, turn signals, light settings (for night time accidents), and the gear lever position of the vehicles
- the condition of each vehicle's wheels and tyres
- for commercial vehicles like buses and lorries, a record of how long the driver was behind the wheel
- problems with roads and lighting
- weather conditions and visibility
- names and addresses of drivers, passengers, and witnesses; the severity of their injuries, and which hospitals they were taken to
- details about where any of the vehicles already removed from the scene have been taken.

Case study: weather effects

On 29 January 2012, traffic was flowing smoothly along the I-75 interstate highway near Gainesville, Florida, USA. Then, at 4.00 a.m., 19 vehicles crashed into each other, leaving 10 people dead and more than 20 injured. When rescuers arrived, the air was thick with smoke from a nearby brush fire. Survivors said the visibility had dropped from crystal clear to nothing in the space of only 15 metres (50 feet). When some drivers slowed down, the drivers following them could not see their cars and ploughed into them.

The mystery was why the smoke was so thick on the road. Meteorologists (people who study the weather) found the answer. Normally, the air at ground level is warmer than the air higher up. However, in an event called a temperature inversion, the opposite happens. Cold air is trapped near the ground by warm air above it. Smoke from a fire usually rises, but on the night of the crash, a temperature inversion trapped the smoke from the brush fire at ground level on the road. The smoke drifted in for several hours, getting thicker and thicker.

Unusual and extreme weather events can create the conditions that lead to serious road accidents like this one.

Tools of the trade

Accident investigators carry a variety of tools and instruments with them to the scene of a road accident. These include:

- a tape measure
- an electronic surveying instrument called a total station that measures angles and distances
- digital still and video cameras
- notepads, pens, and pencils
- a calculator
- a portable computer
- a **GPS** unit.

In addition, investigators might carry electronic instruments that measure the effectiveness of a vehicle's brakes and the slipperiness of the road surface.

Accident investigators draw a sketch of the accident scene. To do this, they might just use notepaper and a pen to make a simple hand-drawn sketch on an accident report form. For a more complex and more serious accident, they might need to use special tools to create a more detailed scale drawing or a computer-generated plan (see page 42).

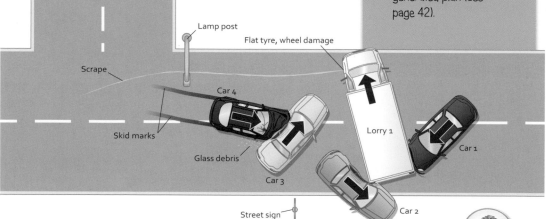

Lamp post

Flat tyre, wheel damage

Scrape

Car 4

Skid marks

Glass debris

Lorry 1

Car 1

Car 3

Car 2

Street sign

Asleep at the wheel

A tired driver is a dangerous driver, and so technology has been created to keep track of driving hours. In many countries, especially in Europe, large commercial vehicles such as buses and lorries must be fitted with a device called a tachograph. It records information including time, speed, and distance covered on a paper disc or a card containing a microchip. In the United States, some vehicles are fitted with a device called an electronic on-board recorder, but most lorry drivers keep a record of their working hours in a logbook. Tachographs, on-board recorders, and logbooks enable authorities to check whether drivers are staying at the wheel too long and becoming too tired to drive safely.

WINDSCREENS

The first vehicle windscreens were made of ordinary window glass, but they produced deadly, razor-sharp pieces when they broke. This was replaced with toughened glass that shattered into lots of small pieces, but it broke easily. In the 1980s, this was replaced by laminated glass, which has a sheet of plastic sandwiched between two sheets of glass. If the glass cracks, the plastic holds it together, but it is more difficult for rescue workers to break quickly.

A laminated windscreen is designed to hold together if the glass breaks. It is also firmly bonded (stuck) to its frame so that it stays in place during an accident and protects people inside the vehicle.

A laminated windscreen has a layer of transparent plastic sandwiched between two sheets of glass.

Glass

Plastic layer

Glass

0.76mm (.030 inch)

2.48mm (.098 inch)

Glass   Plastic

Mapping the scene

Accident investigators can record the precise position of every vehicle in an accident by using a variety of technologies. They can do this by using GPS, the same technology that is used for satellite navigation (see the box). They can also measure the distance between each vehicle and two fixed points, such as streetlights.

A police officer records details of damage to the road surface at the scene of an accident. Damage like this can show where an important event such as a collision took place.

The fastest method of measuring position is using a **laser scanner**. A laser scanner sweeps a beam of light back and forth across the accident scene. The system picks up reflections from the vehicles and other objects and uses them to create a detailed image. This is done from three different positions and the three scans are combined to produce a 3D image. Laser scanning allows investigators to map accident scenes in half the normal time, and it also allows police and emergency services to open roads more quickly.

Satellite positioning

The global positioning system (GPS) enables accident investigators to work out exactly where everything at an accident scene is by using radio signals from satellites in space. The radio signal received from each satellite tells a receiver on the ground how far away it is from the satellite. The signals from four satellites enable the receiver to calculate exactly where it is.

Investigators can measure distances at an accident scene by using a surveyor's wheel. The investigator walks along with the wheel. The number of times the wheel turns multiplied by its circumference (length around the outside of the wheel) gives the distance.

Black boxes

If any of the vehicles have **event data recorders (EDRs)**, also known as black boxes, these are analysed. A lot of cars and lorries have these now. An EDR records **data** including the vehicle's speed, engine throttle setting (which affects the flow of fuel or power), and whether the brakes were applied. This is very useful information for accident investigators.

EVENT DATA RECORDERS (EDRs)

Mechanical data recorders were developed for trains in the 1890s. In the 1930s, photographic data recorders were developed for aircraft. The modern electronic flight data recorder was invented in the 1950s in Australia. Since the 1990s, similar electronic EDRs have been fitted to some cars.

Photographic evidence

Sometimes investigators are not called in until after crashed vehicles have been removed. When this happens, they carry out the same process they would follow at the scene of a crash: they gather information from the crashed vehicles, which in this case will have been stored at a garage until they can be repaired or scrapped. Investigators may visit the scene of the accident, or they may work from photographs.

In addition to still photographs taken soon after the accident, investigators may also be able to use moving pictures as evidence. Major roads and intersections are often monitored by video cameras for traffic management purposes. There are nearly 2 million CCTV (closed-circuit television) cameras in the United States. One of these cameras may have recorded the accident. Even if the accident itself has not been recorded, the pictures may still be useful, because they may show how fast vehicles were going in the moments before the accident.

Accident investigators can use pictures recorded by traffic cameras to calculate the speeds of vehicles.

Safe and sound

Hybrid cars and electric cars are so quiet that it can be difficult for pedestrians to hear them coming, so some manufacturers are adding artificial sounds to these cars to make them easier to hear. They can be made to mimic the sound of a normal petrol or diesel engine. In addition, they can be made to sound a warning when they slow down below a certain speed or when a turn signal is switched on.

TRAFFIC LIGHTS

The first traffic signals were installed outside the Houses of Parliament in London, in 1868. They used a swiveling arm, like a railway signal, lit up by gas lamps at night. Lester Wire invented electric red-green traffic lights in Salt Lake City, USA, in 1912. The first electric red-green traffic lights were installed in Cleveland, USA, in 1914.

Complicated or badly positioned road signs that confuse or distract drivers may be a factor in the cause of an accident.

Analysing the data

After collecting information from the crash scene, investigators now have to make sense of it all and use it to form a hypothesis of why the accident happened.

What causes road accidents?

Three key factors may be involved in the cause of a road collision:

- the driver
- the environment (the road surface, road signs, weather, and visibility)
- the vehicle.

Very few accidents are caused by problems with a vehicle. The road layout or road surface is a factor in a small number of accidents. The most common cause of road accidents by far is driver error. However, few crashes have one single, simple cause. Most crashes are caused by a combination of factors and events.

When a driver brakes hard to try to avoid a crash, the vehicle may skid. Each wheel slides along the ground, leaving a black line – a skid mark – on the road. This mark is important evidence; it gives accident investigators a way to find out how fast a vehicle was going before it started skidding.

Skid marks with square ends show that the vehicle skidded to a stop. Skid marks that fade out at the end show that the driver stopped braking before the vehicle stopped.

Tyre tracks in mud or snow give investigators important information about the vehicle's path.

TYRE MARKS

Several different types of tyre marks might be found at the scene of an accident:

- acceleration scuffs, caused by a vehicle accelerating so hard that its wheels spin
- deceleration marks, caused by a vehicle braking hard enough to stop its wheels from turning and making the vehicle skid
- marks turning left or right, caused by a vehicle sliding sideways
- imprint marks, made when a tyre goes through soft ground, mud, or snow and leaves an impression of its tread behind.

CALCULATING SPEED:
THE SKID-TO-STOP EQUATION

This formula can be used to calculate a vehicle's speed based on its skid marks:

$$S = \sqrt{(255\ k\ D)}$$

S = the vehicle's speed in kilometres per hour
D = its stopping distance in metres
k = a number that depends on the "slipperiness" of the road and the braking efficiency of the vehicle

The "$\sqrt{\ }$" symbol means "square root". The square root of a number is a quantity that when multiplied by itself, gives the number. So, for example, the square root of nine is three, because three times three equals nine. Calculators have a button that lets users find the square root of a number. (See page 34 for more about calculating "k".)

How slippery is the road?

To find out how fast a car was going before it skidded to a halt, the investigator has to know what "k" is in the skid-to-stop equation (see page 33). This depends on the vehicle, the road surface, and the weather. For example, a wet road is more slippery than a dry road. The investigator can find out what "k" is by carrying out a skid test.

Experts drive a vehicle similar to the one involved in the accident along the road and then stop it suddenly, so that it skids. Investigators know this vehicle's speed and measure the length of the skid mark, and then they use the skid-to-stop equation to calculate "k". Then, investigators can use this value for "k" as well as the length of the skid mark made by the vehicle involved in the accident to calculate the speed of the crash vehicle.

Accident investigators test a car's braking performance by carrying out a skid test.

YOU'RE THE INVESTIGATOR!

A car has skidded to a halt at the scene of an accident, leaving skid marks that are 31 metres (102 feet) long. Use the skid-to-stop equation to work out how fast the car was going when the driver started braking. You have carried out a skid test and worked out that k = 1. (See page 33 for the equation, and see page 36 for the answer.)

Case study: cut in two

In 2006, police were called to a road accident on the Pacific Coast Highway in California, USA. They found a Ferrari supercar in two pieces! From marks on the road, investigators worked out that the bottom of the car had hit a bump in the road, which launched the car into the air. It hit a power pole, which cut the car in two. The front half and the back half came to rest 45 metres (148 feet) apart on the ground. Amazingly, no one in the car was seriously injured.

The marks on the road where the car took off and the height of the damage to the pole both showed the car's flight path. This helped investigators to calculate that the car had been travelling at 260 kilometres (162 miles) per hour, or more than 160 kilometres (100 miles) per hour over the speed limit! This was a very expensive accident, as the car was worth about £800,000.

A Ferrari supercar like this one was going so fast that it was cut in two after it left the road and hit a roadside pole.

Skid marks

It is not possible to steer a skidding vehicle, so if accident investigators find skid marks that change direction, this may have been caused by:

- the slope in the road
- a change or defect in the road surface, such as a pothole
- a gust of wind from one side
- a problem with the car's brakes that caused uneven braking
- a problem with a tyre
- part of the vehicle making contact with the road surface
- an impact from another vehicle.

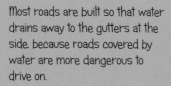

Most roads are built so that water drains away to the gutters at the side, because roads covered by water are more dangerous to drive on.

YOU'RE THE INVESTIGATOR!: THE ANSWER

Look back at the box on page 34.

The skid-to-stop equation is: Speed = √(255 k D)
Putting the numbers into the equation gives: Speed = √(255 x 1 x 31) = 88.9 km per hour

Did you get it right?

Wet and dry

Stopping distances are much longer on wet roads compared to dry roads. A car that stops from a speed of 50 kilometres (30 miles) per hour on a dry road in 24 metres (80 feet) might need a distance of 35 metres (115 feet) to stop from the same speed on a wet road. The reason for this is that the water gets between the road and vehicle tyres, making it more difficult for the tyres to grip the road. Ice is even more slippery and makes it even more difficult for a vehicle to stop without skidding.

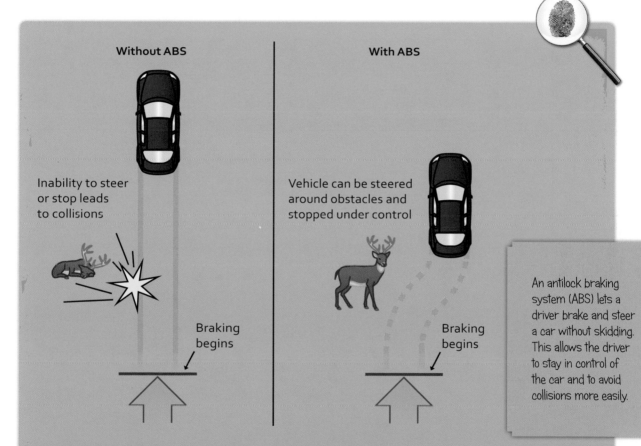

Without ABS

Inability to steer or stop leads to collisions

Braking begins

With ABS

Vehicle can be steered around obstacles and stopped under control

Braking begins

An antilock braking system (ABS) lets a driver brake and steer a car without skidding. This allows the driver to stay in control of the car and to avoid collisions more easily.

Antilock braking system (ABS)

Some vehicles are fitted with a system that stops them from skidding when the driver brakes. It is called an antilock braking system, or ABS. A computer monitors the vehicle's wheels. If any wheels suddenly slow down during braking, they may be about to stop turning altogether and skid. The computer releases the brakes for a moment and applies them again up to 15 times a second – much faster than a human could possibly engage and release the brakes. This stops the wheels from skidding and stops the vehicle in the shortest possible distance.

Pedestrians

The faster a vehicle is travelling when it hits a pedestrian, the more severe the pedestrian's injuries will be. A car does not have to be going very fast to kill a pedestrian. Only 10 per cent of pedestrians hit by a car travelling at about 60 kilometres (40 miles) per hour will survive.

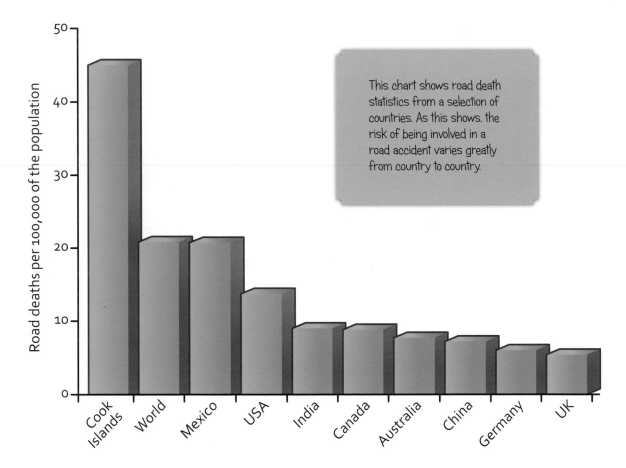

This chart shows road death statistics from a selection of countries. As this shows, the risk of being involved in a road accident varies greatly from country to country.

In the case of a collision with a pedestrian, investigators try to find out:
- where the pedestrian walked onto the road
- the point on the road where the vehicle hit the pedestrian.

A pedestrian's injuries show which way he or she was facing when struck. The height of any injury shows whether or not the vehicle was braking heavily at the time of the impact – because a vehicle's nose dips under heavy braking. The amount of damage to the vehicle and the distance a pedestrian was thrown after being hit indicate the vehicle's speed.

YOU'RE THE INVESTIGATOR!

You are asked to settle a dispute between a driver and a pedestrian involved in an accident. The driver says he braked hard when the pedestrian ran out in front of him, but he could not stop in time. The pedestrian says the car hit him and only then braked. You take measurements from the scene. The bottom of the car's bumper is 45 centimetres (18 inches) above the ground and the injuries on the pedestrian's legs also begin 45 centimetres (18 inches) above the ground. Who is telling the truth? (Find the answer below.)

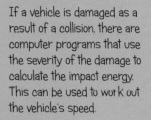

If a vehicle is damaged as a result of a collision, there are computer programs that use the severity of the damage to calculate the impact energy. This can be used to work out the vehicle's speed.

YOU'RE THE INVESTIGATOR!: THE ANSWER

If the driver had been braking hard before the impact, as he said he was, the front of the car would have been forced downwards by the braking action, and the injury would have been lower than the car's normal bumper height. However, the height of the car's bumper and the height of the pedestrian's leg injuries are the same, so the car did not brake before it hit the pedestrian. Therefore, the pedestrian's version of events is correct.

Making plans

After an accident, investigators draw up a scale plan of the scene along with a report of the accident investigator's findings. This may be all that is needed. However, in the case of a serious or particularly complicated accident, investigators might create a computer-generated simulation of the accident. This could be a two-dimensional (2D) **animation** showing the accident happening as if viewed from directly above. Alternatively, it could be a three-dimensional (3D) animation that can be viewed from different angles. This can take several months to produce.

Accidents like this one are traumatic for all involved. People might not remember events correctly or they might dispute what happened. Computer-generated animations of an accident are very useful for showing investigators and courts how an accident happened, and also for confirming calculations made by investigators.

YOU'RE THE INVESTIGATOR!: THE ANSWER

Look back at the box on page 41. The marks and glass on the road show that the car's wheel started scraping along the ground first, and then the collision occurred after this. So, the blowout happened before the crash. A blowout of a front tyre makes a car very difficult to steer, and so this may be the cause of the accident.

Case study: jet crash

On 20 September 2006, Richard Hammond was driving a jet-powered car called a Vampire at Elvington Airfield, for the popular television programme *Top Gear*. He made six successful high-speed runs, but during the seventh run, the car suddenly veered off the runway and turned over at 463 kilometres (288 miles) per hour. Hammond was seriously injured, but he made a full recovery.

Luckily for investigators, the car was being filmed. When investigators watched the film, they saw its front-right tyre blow out just before the car crashed. They believe a small, sharp object pierced the outer casing of the tyre during the sixth run, causing a blister on the tyre that could be seen in the film. It was this weakness in the tyre that gave way and caused the accident.

Hammond reacted instantly and did all the right things. He braked, steered into the skid, and released the car's braking parachute, which shut down the jet engine. However, the accident happened so fast that the car would have crashed anyway, no matter what Hammond did.

In addition to animations, crash tests provide valuable information for accident investigators about the sort of damage vehicles suffer in accidents, because the speeds and directions of the vehicles in the tests are known precisely.

Investigation: reaction time

The time it takes a vehicle to stop is made up of:
- *perception time*: the time it takes a driver to realize that something has to be done
- *reaction time*: the time it takes the driver to start braking
- *braking time*: the time it takes the vehicle to stop.

You can measure your reaction time with a ruler. Ask someone to hold the ruler vertically so that the bottom end is level with your open thumb and index finger. Then ask the person to drop the ruler without telling you when it will happen. When you see the ruler falling, close your thumb and index finger to catch it. The point where you grip it shows how far the ruler has dropped.

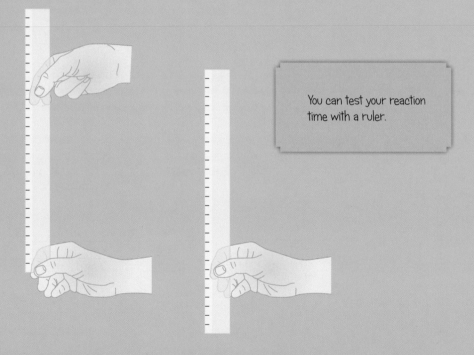

You can test your reaction time with a ruler.

The time, acceleration, and distance of the falling ruler are shown by the following equation:

$$\text{Time} = \sqrt{(2 \times \text{distance}/\text{acceleration})}$$

You can read the distance on the ruler. The acceleration of the ruler is 9.8 metres per second per second. So, if the ruler drops 20 centimetres (or 0.2 metres), your reaction time is:

$$\text{Reaction time} = \sqrt{(2 \times 0.2/9.8)} = \sqrt{(0.04)} = 0.2 \text{ seconds}$$

WHY DO YOU NEED TIME TO REACT?

When a driver sees something, the information travels from the eyes to the brain, which decides what to do. Then, the brain sends out signals to move the hands and feet. The electrical impulses that travel along nerves move very quickly – on average, at about 320 kilometres (200 miles) per hour. But even at this speed, they take a moment or two to travel from the eyes to the brain and back to the muscles. This is the reaction time.

Gliding cars

If water gets between the ground and a vehicle's tyres, the vehicle glides along on top of the water. This is called aquaplaning or hydroplaning. The vehicle's brakes and steering stop working, because there is not enough friction between the road and tyres. This can increase a vehicle's stopping distance by 50 to 70 per cent.

Police officers and some other professional drivers are trained to control a vehicle skidding on wet roads by practising on a special wet surface called a skid pad.

Index